BOOB
EXPLOSION

Charles Chiyangwa

ISBN: 0615384498
ISBN-13: 9780615384498

This book is dedicated to my parents and the whole family. Thank you for allowing me to follow my dreams. I will always appreciate it.

Table of Contents

Humping the pavement.   5
I could not help but admire my sexy
little body.   7
The bitch that cut me.   10
If you are not married you are a slut.   12
The most popular thing among women
is a penis.   13
I am getting a boob job to increase my
guy numbers.   14
Honey you shrunk the booty.   16
I took all my girlfriend's grandma panties
and burnt them.   19
Some women are created by god as a
mistake.   23
Do I get the job or get laid or both?.   25
Married women are porn stars for
one man.   28
My friend is depending on a serial killer.   30
Size matters to toddlers.   32
She is tight between the legs.   32
After prom your days of free sex are
numbered.   34
Beware of your high school teachers.   35

Girls there is enough time to take off
underwear.   36
I slept with cousin Becky.   38
Best dressed crack whore.   39
Lipstick on the wrong lips.   41
I used to call big boobs a dead
man's chest.   42
Janet Jackson we are ready for the
left boob.   43
Oh he is African he is going to bang a
fat white chick.   43
Whatever you do you do not want
to mess up a black man's shoes.   46
You get a group of babies.   49
I fell in love with an armless girl.   51
The lord cannot be in a strip club.   53
I am doing everything she says.   59
Having a penis does not mean that
you are a man.   60
I have been shot!.   61
Come to Texas for the cowgirl
experience.   63
Getting laid by hookers on
Santa Monica Boulevard.   67
Skinny women are easier to fuck.   70
I am a Britney Spears fan.   75
Truth be told some singers are
prostitutes.   77

White girls take care of broke
black men.   78
I am going to take you tiger riding.   86
The fastest pant dropper is 94
Thank you for coming.   94
Hollywood blvd 2.00pm.   95

flash boom!!!

In the hustle and bustle of Los Angeles night life. Hollywood boulevard can be a crazy place. An incident of historical proportion happened right in front of me. On a busy Saturday night I was getting something to eat. As I walked on the walk of fame something caught my eye. I saw what must have been twenty scantly clad babes approaching me. As I got closer to them things started to move in slow motion. They all waved and said hi. I slowly made the first and then the second step passing them. On my third and fourth step I looked back. To my surprise they all looked back in unison. They did it swinging their bodies revealing more flesh. BOOM!. Suddenly they all flashed their boobs at me in unison. It was a good fifteen pairs of double dees.

For the first few seconds I started to tremble. Then my eyes almost popped out. Eyewitnesses say I raised my hands and did a little dance. Other people say I dropped to the ground and started humping the pavement. I have heard

I fainted dropped to the ground and an ambulance was called. The bloggers have said I started doing the hoola hoop motion. Then suddenly started air humping with my hands steering like I was driving a car. I have also heard that one of the girls walked back kissed me and we both fell down. Things are said to have happened on the ground. I have heard that I started speaking in tongues. Rumors has circulated the Los Angeles Police Department has it on surveillance tape. The tape has been classified and will never be released to the public. That worries me even more. To this day my friends have said that my personality was changed forever. I have been accused of not having a social filter. They say I do not talk sense all the time. I have been accused of thinking weird. There was a boob explosion and I do not remember what happened immediately after. To understand what may have happened, I need to explore my relationship with boobs and the people that have them. Boob keepers as I like to call them. It is a daunting task to try and figure out exactly what happened after the boob explosion.

To make things easier I am going to let you know how I feel about things. Maybe you can help me figure out what happened. I will let you be the judge.

The difference between me and the rest of the world is that I saw my own birth. I do not mean from video. I actually opened my eyes during delivery and saw my own birth. As I was coming out the temperature dropped and I cried out. It was right then that I opened my eyes and witnessed my own birth. I immediately had problems. First of all I could have come out much faster. It should not have taken eighteen hours. With that kind of start you start to wonder why I am always late. I know many people think they know what I saw. What they do not know is how the whole thing looks like when you are one minute old or five minutes old. I have photographic memory for god's sake. I was busy crying because it was damn cold and I was naked. I could not help but admire my sexy little body. Even at that age I could tell the world was headed for trouble with me. I just had a feeling of what my future was going to be in this world. That feeling did not last long. I remember the scissors cutting my umbilical cord. I am thinking WTF?. You cut me again there's going to be problems. With the devil look in her eyes I was afraid she was going to cut my leg too. You don't know what rituals these people have. I started thinking about toddler defense mechanisms. I had to find a way to defend myself. When she held my hand up I was like oh my god!. What is life going to be like without a hand?. Please do not cut my hand. I am thinking I just been cut in the middle of my stomach. These people are showing me around like I am some show baby. I am crying and everybody is smiling. Despite the pain I was curious to see the people that had given birth to me. I saw my mom and then my dad. I was like you think you have done something good here?. Of course they did not understand me. I admit I was a bit cranky. It must have been my lost eighteen hours. The more I cried the more I got hit repeatedly from the back. I am thinking I am an infant. They are using violence to shut me up. At this point I was like I am going to run out of here. I tried but I had no strength. I was so weak it sucked bad. I was stuck with these people always looking at me every move. I was getting sick of it.

Let me just say that at this point after nine months, I was glad to be out of the womb. I remember the last two days inside the womb. I wanted to kick the damn thing open. I did kick a few times. The scariest thing inside the womb is that you do not know what to expect when you finally come out. You do not know who these people are. For all you know they could be serial killers. Maybe they are just going through divorce court. My biggest fear was if the pregnancy was a product of rape. I prayed everyday that god please let this be consensual sex. Good old fashioned love making. Part of my anger was that if I was created nine months ago why did it take that long to come out. I did not understand that. People do not understand what happens when you are in the womb. You do not get to choose your own food. I was always like please do not give me the same type of food. The same food appetite that I now know is called cravings. Man those are particularly bad. I am like WTF? I just had this food two hours ago. Have some variety and class lady. Do not disrespect me. I will kick this thing open. Some of the things that happen when you are inside the womb I will not say. Simply put I will take my knowledge to the grave.

People always give credit to the person that delivered them when they were born. To me that nurse is always going to be the bitch that cut me. I feel that way because I looked into her eyes and she cut like she was cutting an animal. I remember looking at her and talking to myself. I can not believe this. Is she for real?. I would have appreciated if she had said this might hurt a little. I was already crying because I was naked and it was cold. I was lucky after a rough start my mom and dad took good care of me. I think I turned out okay. My advice to the new born just coming out is cut your own umbilical cord. Make arrangements prior to coming out. Have your own mom cut it. She will do it with care because you share the pain. I hope I have helped all you knuckle head infants born everyday. I love my mom though. She stuck with me although we had a rough start. This is no joke. No punch line. I love my mom.

I do not understand women. If there was a class called women 101 I failed it.

I have dealt with my misunderstanding of women by laughing. I love women. I love them more when they are naked. I have been told that it is not cool to say. It is not politically correct to say!. I am just being honest. Those dudes that say they love women with turtle necks are liars. When women start taking those clothes off that is sexy to me. You do not have to be a size zero. As long as you drop them pants you are sexy. Being too honest sometimes gets me in trouble. I don't care. It is what it is. What can I say?. A naked lady is much prettier than a clothed one. It is even better in 3D. That is for my brothers that only see naked women in magazines. It is the same with how women think. To women a naked man is sexier than a clothed one too. I have been told this by women. Those women may not be reliable sources. That is because they tell me after I have paid them for sex. They say a naked man is ready. Who knew?. I thought guys were quick enough to get the job done. Guys it you are going to get laid wear a toga with no underwear. That should make it fast and save the ladies some time. I do not want to sound like I am thinking for women. I know your dirty little minds.

I heard that women take a few minutes after they meet a guy, to decide whether they are going to have sex with him or not. Bitches that is too quick. You have to take it easy. At least a guy takes you to eat. Stroll to the house for some tea time. When you take off your clothes that is when I know. I am getting laid!!. That is reasonable time at least. A few minutes is just being a whore. I know women that call each other sluts. That is fun to hear. I am not the one saying it. That is suppose to be hurtful. The question is who is not a slut? I have heard things like serial dater. That is a slut. She goes from one guy to the next. She dates the next guy after breaking up with the first one. That is a slut. She only sleeps with other men when her boyfriend treats her bad. That is a slut. After careful analysis I have concluded that if you are not married you are a slut.

Women do not feel bad for yourselves. Guys that do the same are called Chippendales. Is that right?. Well maybe. Both names have got no respect so I call it even. In fact the most popular thing among women is a penis. They dream about it. They see it in everything like ice cream cones bananas you name it. They dress for it. They hate each other for it. It is said women marry a man but really she is marrying the penis. Basically we do not matter. As long as a man has got a penis he will get married. Some words of comfort for all ugly men out there. There's got to be something good in the world for everybody. I have been told that saying things like that is just digging yourself into a hole. Who cares? Soon word will get around that there is a lonely guy in a hole. Some chick is going to jump in there with me. It never fails. You wonder how all the stupid men out there eventually get married to somebody. How many men have looked for a woman to marry and have died without finding one. There is always that stupid man that marries that stupid girl. They will have stupid sex. It is the best kind of sex. Care about nothing else but the pounding.

Thank god for women in this world. Women have made many things we enjoy today possible. Like guys taking a bath everyday. If it were not for women

I do not think some guys would even get out of bed. It would be a stinky world with guys drinking all day and peeing on themselves. I do not know how many times I have heard the line I am doing it for the ladies. Simply put the vagina gave men a reason to live. I am doing this to impress a girl. Men say it without any shame. At least women try to cover it up. I have heard women say I am getting this boob job for me. In my lifetime I am still to hear a girl say I am getting a boob job for the guys. I am getting a boob job to increase my guy numbers. A girl with big boobs is not a bad thing. Just that when I am talking to you, you know where my eyes are going to be. If there were no women I would not care to find a job. A job to make money and do what. Drink all day sleep all night. It is a good life. That could be a good rap song.

> I am spending all my life trying to impress women so
> that I can get between their legs. In between I go.
> Right through. Are you with me girl. Every time I spend
> my time with you that's all I wanna do babe.

That could be a hit song you never know. I wish there was a better way to say that. All that being said, give it up to the women that put on miniskirts to the club in winter. I wish I knew where they are coming from because I get cold. Without eye candy winter or summer you will not find me in a night club period. I would be at home playing video games.

If I am asked the question what era where you born in? I am not going to say the internet era ,facebook era or myspace era or anything like that. I am going to say I was born in the booty pop panties era. The following explanation is for those of you not familiar with booty pop panties. In case you were living under a cave. These are padded panties that make a woman's ass appear larger. These make it pop out as they say. If you are a woman you have probably worn these. If you are a man your hands have probably felt these in the club. That is where we are now that natural god given buttocks are no longer enough. First it was the thong meant to deceive men that girls are not wearing any underwear. My advice to women is stop the deceiving business.

Do not put on any underwear at all. You do not want to be stuck in a hotel room with a deceived man. Many a time I have found myself asking what happened? Honey you shrunk the booty. Honey you shrunk the boobs. Was that the girl I met in the club? It is frustrating. Stop it.

The task of looking for a partner is easier for men. A quick physical look and men know what it is going to be. Men want to poke every woman they meet if they were given a chance. On the other hand women have to sort out thousands of men who all want to poke them. That is no easy task. Considering that for complete evaluation they have to test drive. After numerous test drives a woman has to ask herself a question. Is this normal or I am just a serial dater?. I am using kind words now. They go through many questions like is he big enough or can I find bigger?. Faced with all these things I would be an emotional creature as well.

A rich man will cheat. If a broke guy cheats on you do not worry about it. He is broke why do you care?. Save your tears. Yes you want to save your tears for when you finally get your rich guy. The fact is rich men cheat. Girls buy yourself a tear bucket. You are going to need it. Maybe I am saying this because I am poor. Who cares!. You see when rich women cheat they look for men with more money than they do. Which basically takes guys like me out of the equation. On the other hand men cheat with anything as long as it has a vagina. If donkeys had vaginas rich men would be sleeping with donkeys. It can be a crack head on the street corner. If she is ready and willing he will do it. Ladies if you smell crack on your man and he has never done drugs in his life, do not worry about it. He is not a drug addict. He is just fucking one. By the time you start asking questions the crack head you are hot about is probably kneeling down on her fifth customer of the night. Picture this, you in your Gucci gown asking questions. It is not going to change anything. I do not want to be mean but you and your Gucci gown are worth the life of a crack head. If it does not make sense to you, well you are fucking the same man. The crack head wins. That is the bottom line with rich men.

Let me just put it out there that I like rich old women. If you are rich and old I like you. I do not care if you got dentures, grandma panties, grand kids and all. I like you. I like you with all your medication. I think we can do some things. For me it's like do not die on me granny. I want to take you back to the moon. That is as long as you are rich. I do not want to be stuck with an unhealthy senior. Healthcare is expensive. I think I got the Anna Nicole syndrome. I know you are calling me a scumbag by now. Do not call me that. I hate that. You can call me a male prostitute that is fine. I am cool with it. Men and women do it everyday. When I do it people start calling me names. I get emotional and stuff. It always leads to tears. As a man you want to be able to do stuff that women do without being called names. It is hurtful. They call me a male prostitute when I am just following my passion which is rich old women. I wish there was a way to do this quietly without the name calling. If an older woman drags a young drunk guy out of the club to her house she is a cougar. When a guy drags a young drunk woman to his house he is a sexual predator. Not that I have done it.

I am just saying. Just making a point. I do not want cops at my house asking stupid questions. When was the last time you did the do?. Like I said I am trying to make a point dumb ass. You are getting me worked up. When I get worked up all hell breaks loose. I am going to say stuff that people are not going to feel good about.

I took all of my girlfriend's grandma panties and burnt them. I took all the lingerie that did not match and burnt it too. Then I staged a fake break in that only targeted her underwear. She come home and wanted to call the police. I offered to buy her new matching underwear all thongs. I am not proud of what I did. Before you condemn me just remember in my mind underwear has to match. That is what you get when you get me worked up. It is not a good idea. The problem with getting me hot is that there are all these things I did when I was in college. Things I am not proud of that have been eating me up. Things bubbling to come out. When I get that feeling I cannot stop.

I remember there was an old widow named Tracy at the apartment complex

I rented in college. Tracy was about eighty years old. Her husband had passed away five years before. Every night we heard lovemaking noises even though no man ever entered her place. Tracy had no boyfriend. This went on everyday and me and my friend decided to find out. When Tracy was out at church we broke into her house and found a bag of sex toys. We took the bag to a friend's house. I had never seen an old lady so angry. She cried all night. This was actual crying she was doing now. I felt sorry for her so I immediately went to retrieve her bag. Come to find out that my friend's girlfriend had already used some of the toys. She had loaned some of them to a neighbor. I spend all night trying to fill up a bag of sex toys. It was three in the morning when I finally got everything. I knocked on Tracy's door and left the bag there. I hope by God these girls did not have any disease or nothing like that. You do not want granny going down with gonorrhea or syphilis. I hope she washed them good before using. I doubt that though. I had not even finished making my cup of coffee when the love making sounds started again. That got me thinking deep down inside I am a good person.

I hear this nonsense about girls wanting to date a fit guy for protection. Okay how about I need to be with a girl that knows kung fu. That is so she can have my back when something goes wrong. If I feel my life can be in danger my girl should be able to defend me. Equal rights just like I am able to protect her. I always tell my woman to put on a tank top knowing her breasts will be popping out in case something goes wrong. I can use her as a shield. No man can punch breasts in a fight. That is what I call boob security. If he does punch and the implants pop out those things can be replaced later.

Doctors are coming up with so many diseases these days. I will not be surprised if one day they come up with a disease called toddler frustration syndrome. This disease will cause toddlers to cry when they wet their pants. It also causes them to cry when they are hungry. Advanced stages of this disease will include scratching the mother for more milk. Is that a disease really?. I know I can find many diseases like that these days. I think some of these diseases is just trying to find a reason to legitimately do drugs. It is just like smoking marijuana these days. You just find a reason to get the medical marijuana card. You just find a reason to get the medical marijuana card. That is if they have not made weed legal already. I am sure you can get one if your feet hurt after walking two blocks barefoot. You can also get one if you have a vomiting problem after drinking too much. The medical marijuana calms you down.

I have black lips and pink lining. My mouth looks like a vagina. I am thinking girls look at me and wonder how I can have such a thing as a mouth. What can I do?. That is the hand that I was dealt. It is not like I can have surgery.

After staying six years with my girlfriend one day I noticed that she had six fingers. I almost dropped dead on the floor. Now I complement a girl's hands and check them out at the same time. You do not want to make the same mistake twice. Six fingers will crypt you out. Now I stare my women from head to toe looking for stuff. I always get asked this question. Hey what are you doing?. I just laugh it off but I continue. I am fascinated by women. It has been hard to figure them out especially American women. I think about women day and night. I also happen to have a job to make people laugh. You can put two and two together. I hope you think I like women because I do. Making fun of women is one thing. That is part of my line of work. Getting laid is another thing. I certainly want to get laid all the time. That is the reason for living. That is why men do not sleep trying to make money. I hope after we are done laughing we get down to business.

Some women are hot literally. I put my body against them and I get hot. I am already sweating without even doing nothing. I feel the heat and that is a good thing. Having said that some of you women are crazy!. You get the feeling that some women were created by God as a mistake. It has nothing to do with looks. They could be as fine as hell. If drama is in their bones you are in for a ride!.

If a push up bra is your salvation it means that your boobs can no longer support themselves. John has been playing with them too much. Being honest it just means your body is starting to break down. If you once had everybody looking now some guys are skipping. If your boobs are covering your abs well that is a situation. A situation that needs to addressed by a surgeon. Women call me the marrying kind. I get to the scene and ask the dreaded question. Where are you going to be in five years? I can see you are not going to be in the club. When she begins to cry I tell her I will marry you. You have never seen a woman happy. I do that because it quiets them down. The marrying kind is not going to get married to some bra worshiping chick. I am looking for the young free standing ones. Those that pop out by themselves. I am not saying all women should have a boob job. That is not what I am saying. What I am saying is that you have to find a way to love yourself. I am just one guy there are millions of other guys that feel different ways. If you try to please all of them you will not make it. Love what you have and somebody is going to love you for it. All you need to get is one guy out of all the millions. Unless you are a whore there is nothing I can do about that.

Of all the hard things god gave men I am glad he did not give us an ugly sex organ.

I have gone to job interviews where the secretary starts flirting with me. The question becomes do I get the job or do I get laid?. Fuck the interview I am getting laid. Then I come to my senses. I am like damn I need the money. If this was a perfect world I would get laid right here on this table like they do in porn movies. Unfortunately this is not a perfect world. The manager who is interviewing me is overweight and he just farted as he passed right by me. Who does that to a guy looking for a job?. He must have had egg breakfast. According to the conversation I am over hearing the secretary is married and has a boyfriend. I am going to get out of other people's business and concentrate on mine.

I was sitting at a sidewalk café on Hollywood boulevard, sipping on a cup of coffee. Across from me was a young beautiful blonde chick sitting at the next table. She flashed her pink underwear with a smile. I was smiling wide too. I was like welcome to America!. Girls in Iowa do not behave like this do they? This happened three weeks after a group of girls flashed their boobs at me. Must have been a strippers night on the town or porn star night out. I remember it was like fifteen or sixteen pairs of double dees. It was a boob explosion. It took me a while to come to terms with what had happened. It was like my two seconds in heaven. The question has always been about the moments after.

I have never been to NASCAR. My pockets are not slim. They are anorexic. That is how poor I am. I could not afford to buy condoms when a hooker offered herself for free. That is not the point. The point is I have never been to NASCAR. I have been in America for more than a decade and I cannot afford NASCAR. That is like spending a decade without having sex but walking around with condoms in your hand. I hope it will happen someday. I live by the 101 Hollywood freeway.

The next best thing is to climb down the Hollywood freeway at western. They have a bus stop on the freeway. I go down there on a Saturday or a Sunday at eight in the morning. It feels like the real thing. Watching cars doing eighty to a hundred miles an hour is exhilarating. My adrenalin is pumping and I am cheering them on. One guy saw me and he did a loop. He come back the second time driving a Ferrari. That has to date been my best experience. When I go down there I always put on a suit. If you go wearing any other clothes people automatically assume you are homeless. I have to wear a designer suit that was donated to me by some rich folks. I do not have anywhere else to wear it to. A guy wearing a designer suit cheering cars on the freeway at eight in the morning makes quite a sight. When I get home from the freeway, I just say to myself some people are rich. I only do this at the weekend. I tried doing it during rush hour traffic on a weekday. That was a disaster. I got down there it was like a parking lot with bumper to bumper traffic. I had never seen people so angry. People were swearing from everywhere.

They were so angry they started taking it on me. Some guy said to me hey get a job. I have a job dumb ass!. I just come down here because I thought you would be speeding. Well since your dumb ass is stuck down here in traffic I might as well head home. If by this time you have missed the point here it is again. I cannot afford NASCAR.

I have never understood why people get married. The way it was explained to me was shady. The way I experienced sex was the same with most women with variations. That was until last night. I met a girl from Texas. Lord! things where done to me. At the end of it I did not remember my name. Finally I understood why men get married. You get something that you know is going to be hard to find. It is so good that you want it everyday. You imagine yourself living this kind of life with no interruption. Some women are so good at sex they are like porn stars. I do not want to say that all married women are like porn stars. I am strongly leaning towards that direction. I know I am going to be condemned for it. Married women are porn stars for one man. I hope that sounds better and will stop all the nonsense against me. They are porn stars for one man. That made me understand marriage. What a ride!.

I stopped giving advise to people because it always turns out to be bad advice. I praised a girl that had just bought a new car. I told her this line. It is not what is between your legs, it is what your legs are driving that matters. She immediately flipped it on me with this line. For men it is not what your legs are driving, but the size of what is between your legs that matters. At that point I was like that is not what my girlfriend told me. I gave advise to a young girl. I told her to do all the things that the boy she liked wanted to do. I said it would be a good start. She is now pregnant. What a start!. I advised a good friend of mine to be honest and true to himself. He told his manager that she was fat and that she needed help to save her life. He told her that she looked like a useless stump of flesh. My friend's manager started going to the gym and turned her life around. She looks fine as hell now. Well my friend was fired on the spot. I saved a life but my friend is now homeless. I bring him food once in a while. It is life. It is what it is. There are consequences for every decision you make. Every time I tell this story everybody is angry at me. Why are you not helping your friend?. Life is not a movie where everything ends good and everybody is happy. Before you judge me here is the question. How many homeless people have you helped?. There is something that I had been leaving out in the story. I am going to say it now. I know my friend has it in him to succeed. If only he can give up cocaine he will be just fine. Until then I am going to continue dropping off lunch once in a while. I know all of you have someone in your life you wish you could help. You know it is impossible to make it work. It is heartbreaking. I am not one to tell you to be strong and hopeful. I am not strong. I have shade tears for my friend many a time. I wish they were tears of joy. I hope the next time I shade tears for him, it will not be at the cemetery to pay him my last respects. If you date a serial killer he may end up killing you. It sounds obvious but I know women that have married serial killers in prison. My friend is depending on a serial killer. God help him.

I was going about my business with my girlfriend. In my own bedroom when suddenly milk started coming out of her breasts. My eyes almost popped out. I could not believe it. It took me back to the last time I breast fed way back when. I had to taste this milk. You can understand it had been a while. The milk still tasted good man. I made good work of the chance and by the time she left one breast was bigger than the other. Going back to the last time I had tasted breast milk. It was a traumatic event. Somehow people felt that I was grown up enough that I had to start eating real food. You know me I was not having it. I was not going to stop easy. It got to a point when they had to make me stop. They shouted it and I just pretended like I did not understand what they were saying. I was young you know two or so years old. They started putting the hottest spice on the breast. Every time I tried to get milk it burnt my mouth. It was horrible. By the time they offered the third time I refused. That is how they got me to stop breast feeding. My mom was cool it was this other evil lady that was telling her what to do.

Boobs are the most interesting part of a woman's body. Think about when you were born a few days after the first cry. You are already looking around for boobs trying to figure out whether you have big ones or small ones to drink milk out of. You do not want to run out of milk you know. At that age you cannot do anything for yourself. Size matters to toddlers. If every time you try to breast feed your child and he/she pees. Clearly they are not happy with the breast size.

This world could be a better place if people were honest. When you ask a person a simple question they lie in your face. Somehow it is accepted under the disguise of political correctness and or being polite. For example when you ask a man a simple question. Why did you marry your wife? Instead of telling the truth they use all kinds of words to describe her. She is beautiful, sensual, sensitive and so on and so forth. Instead of going straight to the point. She is tight between the legs. I am not going to use the p word. I am not about that. She has tight p.........I did not put it in there you did. I know your dirty little mind is working overtime.

It is noon and I am sitting at a sidewalk cafe on Hollywood boulevard. I was staring for a minute. I become dizzy and my imagination started running wild. I get conscious and start to see the cars again. It gets dizzy again and my imagination goes into overdrive. I could hear the crowds. At this moment I was not sure what they were waiting for. I imagine this could be like five thousand people packed in an arena at night. A thumbing drum and bass rhythm rocking the stage. A projected multimedia screen showing images sentimental to me serves as the backdrop. House lights go out leaving only the stage lit. Then I stumble onto the stage. The crowd notices me and they give a good round of applause. I could see the last person fly in and slowly settle down.

My name is Charles Chiyangwa and I am from Africa. I may be from Africa but the fundamentals of my body are strong. Otherwise I could not be able to make love. I can see the Hollywood sign from my house and that qualifies me to be in a movie. I am in a movie titled Robbin' In Da Hood. Now if you are a black man and you have a check with Robbin' In Da Hood written on it. There is going to be some problems. I had problems cashing the check after I did the movie. They had to call the producer to verify whether I was an actor or somebody trying to rob the bank. After it was all cleared up, I heard the bank manager tell the police to go back as the matter had been solved. Look I am not a coherent guy. I don't go from point A to point B and so on and so forth. I tend to go off any direction I want. That is the way I think and that is the way I live my life. Therefore I am just going to throw my stories at you and see if we can get some laughing going on.

Free advice for teenagers. After prom your days of free sex are numbered. Soon you will have to pay for food on a date with money you have actually worked for. Just like everybody else. Sometimes you get something at the end of the date. Other times you have to go on few dates. Spending money that you actually worked for to get something. I think that is why young fellows tend to be violent when they walk away empty handed. Going Dutch on dates sounds good in principle. At the end of the date girls tend to withhold benefits.

Back in Africa when I was in the eighth grade I did not have shoes. My parents could not afford to buy me a pair of shoes for school. The cute girls with shoes did not want to have anything to do with a boy without shoes. I had to look for girls without shoes like me. That was a challenge. The few that had no shoes were all plus size. That is where I honed my expertise handling big girls. Let me put it in context. You do not want to date a girl that drives a Mercedes when you drive a fifteen year old Ford Taurus. By the way that was my first car. To me it's like you have no shoes bro find girls without shoes.

Beware of your high school teachers. Your teachers are getting crazier every year. Boys if your female teacher keeps kneeling down in front of you that is not good. Her mouth is too close to the young engine. These young engines tend to go off with the slightest provocation. Even the warmth of the teacher's breath close to the engine can set it off. Once that happens the next time you see the pair will be on Television. Girls if your male teacher wants to give you a mammogram after class that is not good. I used to give mammograms after class in my day. I was not teaching anybody. I just gave them to girls I liked. Guys if your girlfriend tells you let's go catch some birds in the woods. Just know that not much bird catching will happen. A lot of humping will probably happen so be prepared. Don't do like I did. I went out there wearing underwear with holes. After that she bought me two packs of brand new underwear. I was poor okay it was not my fault. These days girls are going Britney. That is leaving your underwear at home when going to the woods with a guy. That is too ready. Girls there is enough time to take off underwear. A guy can wait.

Never walk in on your parents. That will traumatize you for life. Do not worry if people make fun of you because you have a long tongue. That will come pretty handy later on in life. Not that somebody will measure it or anything like that. There will be people pleased you have it. A long tongue has given me one of the most memorable moments in my life. You get to see things up close in high definition. I guess we can just leave it there. If you are going to pee in the bath tab at least wait until you are done bathing. Otherwise you are just bathing in your own pee. Do not feel too bad when girls dump you in high school. Just wait a few years when they have kids and they are out of shape. Drive by and say hey do you remember me the nerd?. I am going to the playboy mansion. Meanwhile she will be struggling with them kids running off and stuff.

Parents are control freaks and I mean that in a nice way. That is because kids with their free minds want to do whatever comes to their empty heads. A kid would want to blow up a neighbor because they do not like them. You cannot blame the kid. If you do not like someone you should have the right to blow them up right. The kid's argument is that he blows people up everyday and cut their limps in a video game. So why not do it to an annoying neighbor?. Well it is putting technology to good use right. That is where parenting comes in. The parent has to knock it inside the kid's head that it is not cool. Sometimes parents are too late. When a kid walks in with excitement and announces dad I slept with cousin Becky. At this point it is too late. The real task is to try and make cousin Becky keep her pants on. The lessons of wiener control were late here. The boy had to be taught before hand that his wiener cannot poke everything in a dress. They have to teach him the idea of poking strangers he pretends to know. They have to set the rules. You cannot poke grandma!. You cannot poke your sister. You cannot poke at church. Then they have to lay the last and the hardest one to follow for young boys. Do not poke your teacher.

A friend of mine asked me to dog sit her puppy. She left me with some money to buy her dog's favorite food. I wanted to go cheap. I went to a ninety nine cent store and bought some cheap dog food. I did not buy the brand names she had given me. I tried to feed the dog he wasn't having it. He smelt it and shook his head and lay down there not eating. I had to go buy the brand names before her puppy could eat. This dog was something. When it come time to take the puppy to her home, she refused to leave without the dog food she had refused to eat!. My friend then told me a lot of people had tried to do that to her. We always take the cheap stuff with us. In Africa dogs eat leftover stuff and sometimes there is nothing left. They have to lick bones and they still survive. Out of curiosity I tried to find out if her dog ate the cheap stuff later. My friend told me her dog never eats cheap stuff. She donates it to less fortunate dogs. Okay that ends the story for me right there. That is it. I will leave it right there for now.

I have always wanted to host an award show for the people by the people. This award show will reward ordinary people. Everyday people anywhere you can find them. I hate the idea of waiting the whole year before rewarding people. I will call these awards the street awards. The people will receive awards in the following categories.

Best ghetto booty.
Best ghetto booty by a white girl.
Best ghetto booty by a Latina.
Best dressed crack whore.
Pimp of the year award.

Best walk by a man.
Best walk by a woman.
Best homeless guy.
Happiest guy award.
Best crack head who can keep a job.
Craziest ordinary man in Hollywood.
Craziest ordinary girl in Hollywood.
Player of the year award.
Slut of the year award.
Porn mom of the year award.
The next Armenian American big booty award.

I know there will be a lot of critics of these awards. They will argue that it rewards bad behavior. I think the best ghetto booty needs to be celebrated. Even white guys like ghetto booty. The onion ghetto booty is a classic. The award stays. Best ghetto booty by a white girl needs to be rewarded too. This allows brothers to date across racial lines without giving up their love for booty. Whatever race you are it looks the same from the back. That is absolutely not true. All girls are the same. If that were true there would be no cheating. Best ghetto booty by a Latina. I am just going to say remember Jennifer Lopez!. Now Kim is embedded in our brains. Best dressed crack whore. Who doesn't love a nicely dressed crack whore. Especially if they put on the new bikini jeans. Look on the bright side your friends will think you live in a nice neighborhood. It makes it look good for the two bucks you will spent to get laid. Talk about a bang for your buck!

Here is something that I do not understand. Women spend a lot of time making themselves look good. They have created a billion dollar makeup industry putting lipstick on the wrong lips. I hope one day somebody is going to do it right. Gone are the days of romantic language. He swept me off my feet. Now it is like we hooked up last night. Which basically means we had sex last night. We have narrowed it down to the actions of the actual sexual organs. They are the ones that hook up during sex. What happened to like we were watching the stars last night. We were looking at beautiful roses in the garden under the moon light. People get back to your romantic ways!.

That reminds me of when I was walking the sidewalk on Melrose avenue. I overheard a guy beg his girlfriend to take him back. She asked him why? He told her point blank you blew my head off. Really you blew my head off. I did not know that a guy's head could be blown off by a woman. Obviously it is not his actual head because he was still alive. It is the other head dummy. I hate it when people do not understand simple stuff. If you cannot understand a guy's head being blown off, can you solve an equation?. I think one of my friends had his head blown off by his wife. This is so because no matter what his wife did to him he kept going back to her. At one point he found her in bed with another man. She told him they were shooting a movie and he believed her. They are still together to this day. Obviously his head was literally blown off by this woman. You cannot think without a head right.

Men in America are obsessed with big boobs. In Africa because of A.I.D.S I used to call big boobs a dead man's chest. Women in Africa breast feed in public. I grew up seeing those big ones in buses, trains and it was no big deal. I got to America when I see a woman with big boobs now I get excited. What is happening to me?. I think it is the plastic they are putting in them that makes them big round and bouncy. When those things bounce the push up bra holds them up lord have mercy. I got to snap out of it. I get caught up. Don't blame me, blame them surgeons. Janet Jackson we are ready for the left boob. I just had to get that out of my system. Just show up in the stands or at the tailgate party at next year's Super Bowl and do it.

My name is Charles Chiyangwa and I am from Zimbabwe Africa. I am tired of being profiled. Oh he is African he is going to bang a fat white chick. Look I am banging everybody. Oh he is African he does not go down on women. Oh he is African he is controlling. The only thing I control is your legs bitch!. Oh Africans don't allow you to do anything. Let's just say I am a different kind of African. The one that is going to take you to heaven. African heaven, you never heard of that ha, try me.

Things I would like to talk about. There are fewer brothers in prison for now because Latina gangs are killing them off from the inside. More women are wearing pants now because with those tiny thongs you never know what might end up on the floor. That is out of line. Sometimes I wish this could stop. Somebody help me remember what happened!!!. I am cool. I am going to be fine.

Like everybody in Los Angeles I have been stopped by the Los Angeles Police Department. The officers spend thirty minutes checking my stuff out found nothing on me. He gave me a ticket for having tinted windows.

Many people I know claim to be looking for a job. I don't have a problem getting one because I am not very picky about it. I got a job at the market and I thought I was going be a cashier. Nope!. He gave me a job selling oranges at the freeway entrance. I said no way. After spending all my money at the strip club I was selling oranges at the freeway entrance. When people say you are funny that's another way of telling somebody you are ugly.

My love affair with small town America is undeniable. I lived in two small towns prior to moving to Los Angeles. My very first day in America I was in upstate New York in a small village called Alba. My host took me to a restaurant to eat. I had never seen so many white people eating together. It must have been like hundred or two hundred my numbers could be wrong. I know I just saw a lot of white people. They seem very nice and surprised at my presence. As the only person of color I started looking for all the exit signs in case something went wrong. With so many white people looking at me I could not eat. They had to give me a doggy bag. It was the first time I had ever heard of a doggy bag. Where I come from there were no leftovers period. On a lighter moment one of the women came over to our table to touch my brittle African hair. She spent a little bit of time on it. I got aroused that was kind of embarrassing. The city of Batavia was kind to me for the most part. My hosts took me on a ski trip to Glen Falls New York. I remember sitting on a frozen Lake George. Then come the interesting time to do the skiing. I thought we were going to maybe ski down a little hill a couple of times and that would be it. We spent the whole day skiing. I had never seen so many white people happy. I enjoyed the skiing for the most part. I got involved in a couple of accidents then I called it quits. I was in Batavia New York for about six months. I spent most of my time in Clarendon Texas. That is where I eventually went to school and graduated with the cowboys.

As an actor I have been fortunate enough to travel the world. I love London. The thing about London is that you cannot substitute it with any other place in the world. The atmosphere is just so good and different. You have to be in London to feel it. The British have been made fun of because they have messed up teeth that's okay with me. If you want to look like the mouth of a crystal math addict that is cool with me. Women from Europe have been made fun of because of failing to shave their hairs. If someone wants to look like a monkey that is okay with me. The British must learn to pick up after their dogs though. The pavement is not a dog lavatory bathroom. They messed up my expensive shoes. Four pairs of my expensive shoes with dog poop. Whatever you do you do not want to mess up a black man's shoes. As of now I am still waiting for an apology from the queen. I think the government must do something. Pass a law if they haven't already done so. Pick up or you lose your dog. If your dog messes the pavement we mess you up. To give you an idea how bad the problem was for me in London, I had to walk looking down at the pavement to protect my shoes. I had made up my mind that if dog poop messed up my fifth pair of shoes, I was going to call the police to investigate. The British are very nice people. If you can understand what they are saying when you first meet them.

In Venice Italy it is against the law to feed pigeons. The reason being that the birds were dropping poop on their historic buildings. I think the birds were dropping on a lot of politicians during lunch hour. This in turn caused a lot of traffic to the dry cleaners. After all who can listen to a politician with bird poop on their designer suit. If you have been pooped on by a bird your political life is over!. They fought back passing legislation against birds. Really. I think there is need for a bird protection agency. The rights of birds should be included in the constitution. Flying around is hard as it is. Denying birds food is out of line.

In Paris France they have these unisex public restrooms. The first time I went in there and a woman followed right behind me I froze. All the pee that I had to come out was gone. I just stood there and listened to the sounds of the girl using the stall doing her business. I would really like to describe what I heard. Most people have said it is like giving yourself a death sentence. Do not do it. I will not say nothing until another girl cheats on me. There will be no stopping then. It took me a while to get used to the sights and sounds of that ordeal.

In Johannesburg South Africa they have urinals outside in public. If you have to go you just go by the wall do your business and hop onto the minibus. How convenient this is in the middle of Johannesburg. The city I call a smaller version of New York City. I hope these things will have been changed the next time I visit.

I do not understand why broke people should be allowed at shopping malls. We allow broke people to wonder around the mall and then cry foul when they rob the place. Why should a broke guy with access to a gun be allowed near a bank. That is like allowing a single guy access to a group of naked girls locked up in a room. You get a group of babies. If you have five dollars to your name in an account you should by law stay home. The only thing you should be allowed near are crack whores. You probably have enough money to spend on them. If I am broke I stay home and I never got into any trouble.

Back in Los Angeles my day was crazy as hell. It started off at a gym in Hollywood. I got into the shower and I was the only one without an erection. I was like what is up with that. It was like I had walked into the Los Angeles county jail shower. You would think they have liquid soap by now so that people do not have to bend over. It would be nice for inmates to say I am not bending over bitch.

At Venice beach a dude tried to sell me his underwear. It was clear the underwear had been worn before. The color was kind of white turning brown. I told him if I bought them he would have no underwear. The world is better with him wearing underwear.

I have been told drinking girl urine is a popular fetish. People please! I remember one angry guy hackled me at a club. He was like "what is the big deal man it is mostly water". Of cause it is water that is not for human consumption. It sounded like I was watching an episode of the reality show fear factor. Anywhere I do not think fear factor would work in African villages. Word will quickly spread that Americans were giving free lunch. I have been dating here and I tell you it has been one hell of a cultural experience. I have been asked to eat all kinds of stuff. Girls why don't we stick to eating expensive food. When those legs open its lunchtime for me. I got worried about this and called my parents about it. They hung up on me. After my girl gave me numerous ultimatums, I must say I have started taking frequent trips downtown. My girlfriend is 300 pounds! Yes three hundred pounds. Do not feel sorry for me. I can handle it. Before I go down on her I prey that she does not get too excited and squash my head between her legs. If that happens I know I will not survive. If god asks me "What happened to you". I will try and turn it on him. Your honor it happened exactly as you planned it. You are an awesome God. What a way to go. I know he might try to send me to hell. I won't go without a fight.

I am now living in a neighborhood where I cannot drive slow. If I do all kinds stuff starts happening outside. Women in mini skirts/short shorts start to walk towards my car. Guys in leather suits come to me. "I run shit here" he said. Yes you do. I told him that it was rare that a brother like him would admit to living a shit life. I had to speed away of cause.

Last week I went to Venice beach Los Angeles and at the drum circle somebody passed on a joint to me. Before you know it I was singing kumbaya dancing bare foot on the beach. I started thinking when I fall in love with a girl can she go hunting. Can she kill a lion?. That is just me being African. Where am I?.

I fell in love with an armless girl. True!. She had no arms something happened to her in an accident. That is not the point. It is the kind of sex I had. I tell you ladies chop those arms off you don't need them. You can do so much better without them. I know all of you are thinking owe that is wrong. I insist arms are an obstruction to real bedroom action. Try it with duck tape. Stick them suckers to her body and have the time of your life. I told the trick to one guy and he wanted to buy me a car. Just wanted to let you know. I got enough cars now.

I met a girl and she started telling me I was handsome and all that jazz. I tried to tell her you are mistaken. Think deeply again and see if I am your Denzel or Brad. She said yes I was her prince in shining amour. Women hear me out. Stop making those kinds of mistakes. It will ruin your life.

When god calls me I am not going to do it like everybody else. When he calls them they say nothing and before you know it they are dead. I am not going out without a fight. When he says Charles it is time to go. I am going to tell him no. I am not going nowhere. I am not going out like a punk. That is how we do it in the hood.

I hear if you do that somebody just drives by and shoots your ass. I am going to try it though. Sometimes the drive-by shooting people miss. I am going to just give a stupid excuse. Let me get some ice cream. I will be back in a minute. Disappear for hours to a strip club until God tracks me down again. He cannot come into a strip club right. Yeah I think so. The lord cannot be in a strip club. It is a place for us sinners.

I was reading the Harry Potter book in MacArthur Park near downtown Los Angeles. The park is known for all kinds of bad things. A police officer stopped me and started asking me some questions. What brings you to the park? I told him I was reading Harry Potter. A barrage of questions followed. "A Blackman reading Harry Potter in the park why". "Who is Harry Potter tell me what kind of drugs he does" I told the officer he was out of line. I ended up apologizing for being out of line at the police station. I should have grabbed his nuts and held on to them. Then give the excuse that I was falling and it was the only thing I could hold on to.

I am from Africa! I know. It amazes me that Tarzan is a white guy. In Africa there are not many white people. In Nigeria there are about hundred and fifty million black people. They do racial profiling there. They profile white people. Here is the most popular question they ask a white person. Are you looking for oil? You got white rappers doing police brutality songs to bring out what is happening in their communities. Forgive me I get carried away.

I fantasize about having sex with the A-List movie stars on the beach. Yeah that is just me being me. Why not?.

I remember 911 differently. It was a horrible day but it was also the day I had the most number of boobs pressed on my chest amidst the crying. The big plastic ones made the most impact. They made me think at least for a second oh! oh! here we go again. I must say single handedly it made me cope better with the horrible tragedies of that day.

What's the fuss with the red carpet? I got my own red carpet at the back of my car. You just get to were you want to eat and lay it down then walk through. The only downside is that it takes a while to get to eat. I feel sorry for women in Hollywood. It is difficult to get a good man as it is. What is going to happen now that men are lining up to have sex changes to become women? It is now common to hear a crying woman saying, "She used to be my husband". I did not know that having a period, menopause were that much fun. God I am out of line here. As much as I love talking I wish I could just stop myself from saying certain things. Women are taking a knock today. Do not get me wrong. I love women. You are on my mind all the time so it fits that I write a lot of jokes about women. Make fun of the ones you love type thing. Times are changing. We have the first black president. That is no joke I had to put it out there.

I come to America because I failed to achieve the African dream. Thus to have fifteen wives sixteen children and a lot of cattle. To be honest with you my penis could not handle fifteen wives.

Have you noticed that in the name of security there are cameras everywhere? I do not buy the security argument. They want to know how you were killed. They will be saying see how he got shot. The guy that did it was hiding behind a tree. Meanwhile you are dead. They are going to make a television show out of your dead ass. It will be a reality show called SHOOTING SOMEBODY ON CAMERA; CRAZY,CLEVER OR PLAIN STUPID. VOTE ONLINE.

When I was coming to America my dad was worried about violence in Los Angeles. He gave me a bow and arrow just in case he said. When I got to Los Angeles I saw a guy holding two guns he seemed surprised by my weapons. Meanwhile I was close to wetting my pants. I had to say something. I politely said, "Those guns are beautiful". What was I suppose to say?.

Things are so expensive here in America. I am broke I cannot even afford to die. If you don't believe me try dying and see how expensive it is. That was a pretty dumb joke. I did an audition here in Hollywood they told me that I was not black enough or African enough. All this time I thought I was African and black. The only way to get rid of this problem is to use a white man's picture to get the audition. When you show up they will be like is that you?. You are black!. To that I will say you got it right this time. I am black and I was born in Africa. My only wish is if the highway patrol can make the same mistake. He is not black enough let him go.

I went to Holland and they have whore houses and prostitutes at the shopping window. Thus in the red light district not at the prime minister's residence or anything like that. When I was there it was busy season people were lining up to get some ass. You know me I was not going to stand in line. I am too smart for that. On the other side of the road I could see an old prostitute. Nobody was hanging around there. That made me smile. Now I had my own prostitute without them suckers breathing behind my neck. Never mind the sagging breasts, wrinkled skin a woman is a woman. I went inside and she had a lounge of old men waiting with Viagra in their hands. Now you know why grandpa is no longer giving good advice anymore.

I could not ride a motorbike. It has nothing to do with the fact that I am scared. I know they are fast on the freeway and all. I hate the position you're in when you are riding this thing. It is a sexual position. It feels like a girl waiting to be fucked from the back. Some women love the position because it makes them start thinking about using a strap on in your ass. Here I go again thinking for women. Women do not like it when I talk about their thoughts. Believe me special privileges have been withheld from me after making jokes about this stuff. Think twice when your girl says she enjoys watching you ride. The devil is in her thoughts. For men that like strap on action I am not dissing you. It is going to be okay.

Parents teach your kids about sex. Nobody taught me. Nobody sat me down about having sex. I just went about it myself. My first time was with a girl I knew in the neighborhood. During the sex I could not handle the smell. I almost threw up. I also had drunk a gallon of orange juice to prepare myself. I must admit I had a little tummy going in. I went to my dad and told him the experience. He gave me some advice. He said "Son you have to close your eyes and hold your breath and do it. That is how we all do it". His advice may have worked. I am still single.

I am having problems with my girlfriend. She gave me an ultimatum. She said it is either we go to a shrink for counseling or you do everything I say. I am doing everything she says.

I am tired of people blaming Hollywood for their violent kids. There is violence in ice hockey and football. In ice hockey they fight while crowds cheer.

There has been a lot of wild fires in Southern California. I see a lot of white people living up in the mountains where the fires are happening. My message to white folk is come down white people we are safe. The president is black now. Things have changed down here. There are no fires down here. Come back and get your jobs. Black people cannot do all your jobs. Moving on. The first time I saw one of the houses burning was on television. I was like how did you get up there, let alone build a house?. Say what you may about the bushman, building a house on a mountain is a no no.

I was walking on Sunset Boulevard In Hollywood. I saw a guy wearing leather pants a tight black shirt with wings on the back. I was like does this guy know that no matter how you get high on cocaine or marijuana, nobody has been able to fly. My journey on the sunset strip in Hollywood I saw a lot of beautiful women handsome men and lots of people in between. Finding out people's identities can be an adventure of a lifetime. You know this if you have tried. In Los Angeles having breasts doesn't mean you are a woman. Having a penis does not mean you are a man. This is so because you can have both a penis and breasts. There you go let the search begin and good luck.

When it comes to women my slogan is "a woman is a woman anything is possible". I have been accused by my friends of having low standards when it comes to women. My other slogan did not help. "As long as you can spread them I am cool"

Coming from Africa I imagined I was coming to America this high tech world. I ended up in a small Texas town called Clarendon. There are more cattle than people. I used to have nightmares about cattle ransacking the town killing everybody. I would wake up shouting "They are coming!". "They are coming!". That is a lot different from nightmares I am having now in Los Angeles where I live. I woke up shouting "I have been shot somebody call 911!".

My idea of America was in a big city chilling with all these rappers I had seen on television. There are very nice people in Clarendon Texas. I just think they drink too much beer. Their kids drink even more beer. They drink a lot of beer and prey a lot. Prey to God nothing happens literally. In this small town of about two thousand people there are about fourteen churches. Clarendon a small town of good mannered people. There is nothing to do though. I usually killed time by doing my favorite pass time. That was counting cars on highway 287. I remember one Saturday I had five thousand eighteen wheelers and seven thousand cars. Then I counted ten thousand pick up trucks and five overload trucks carrying houses. I got a kick out of it. Look at it this way. You can only watch so much porn.

Imagine coming from Africa straight to Clarendon Texas then Los Angeles. I had the biggest cultural shock of them all. When I got to Los Angeles, for the first time in my life, I could not tell whether I was looking at a man or a woman. The result was a long stare so I had to ask. What are you? The person replied don't worry honey I am the whole package. Some of the people I met were transgender. Some of them were just plain ugly women with too much make-up on. It took me a long time to get a date in Los Angeles. Long enough to land the nickname date impaired. I got tired of asking my friend about his dates like I cared. I had to lie to get my first date. I said I am a prince the son of a king in Africa. Then suddenly I was cool. That is how I got laid for the first time in Los Angeles. Sometimes I just pretended to be gay and the girls will get all cuddly with me. I am an actor I can be anyone. Then bang I strike. The next morning the girl would say but I thought you were gay. With a smile on my face I would say, "Well you thought wrong". It worked fine all the time except one time I did it to a kung fu instructor. First of all I did not know her kung fu background. The next morning as I smiled to do my line she hit me. She did not stop until I started crying. Now I am more careful. I ask a lot of questions about physical strength and fitness before pulling any of that stuff again.

When I was on my way coming to America my mom warned me. She said do not let the American girls get to your head. I was like it will never happen mom. I got here got laid by a cowgirl. Good lord! I wanted to call mom and tell her about it. "They are in my head the girls". I think Texas should have cowgirls as their state symbol. The slogan should be come to Texas and get the cowgirl experience. You never go back. Another good one would be come to Texas where cowgirls run wild. Try this one; cowgirls will have you wanting more of Texas. While I was living in Clarendon I worked at the gas station. I met a lot of older folks. A lot of them had lived in the same small town for sixty plus years. Some of them had never been to a big city. Most of them had never been out of the country. Now I know. They got tied down by them cowgirls. I do not blame them one bit. The cowgirls almost got me. I guess I am the one that got away.

I get annoyed when women buy sex toys. I got the African jumbo right here and it is free. Women like what they see on television and it is not me. I did not even make the cover of my own movie. Try living like me in Los Angeles and you will write a horror movie. That movie will make a horror master shake his head. Los Angeles has the most handsome homeless people in the world, except me when I was one of them. When I was struggling to find a place to stay, I had problems finding homeless women. They are rare because men with homes are busy fucking them. Hands up if you have never taken advantage of a homeless girl. I got in trouble with my buddies when I used to do stand up. They accused me of being too honest and talking about stuff that affect lots of our own. I said it anyhow. Whatchu you going to do ha!!! .

In Africa it is desirable to grow old because we think you grow wiser and you earn respect. Here in America you got the anti-aging institute. Like growing old is a disease.

Women are always telling me things I do not have. You do not have dimples. Your lips are too big. This one girl said something that stuck with me. She told me she liked men that were hairy. Upon hearing that I started growing hair on my chest, and a whole lot of other places you know what I mean. Everything was fine until she called me an African monkey. Trying to get back at her I called her sexy tiger. She liked it so it did not work. I discovered that you can call women sexy anything and they will like it. Try it. Hey sexy zebra. Hey sexy lizard. Hey sexy Margot. Hey sexy baboon and so on and so on. They will love it as long as it starts with sexy.

The future of transport and safety will include boob friendly seatbelts. Porn stars are complaining that the current seatbelts are uncomfortable. There is also the fear of losing breasts implants in case of an accident. Somebody has to invent a bra that can be connected to seat belts. This will definitely solve the problem.

People in this country are honest. Okay some of you. Last week a hooker passed away and friends and family put up an epitaph that said, At Last She Sleeps Alone. In giving the eulogy the pastor said, "I know most of you have had a piece of this meat". When I first got here I went to a casting agent wanting to get started in the movie business. She told me that my lips were too big and that I needed to go under the knife to get work in this town. Before I left I also thought it was my duty to tell her what she needed. Instead I just stood there and cried.

During the summer women in Los Angeles turn heads. My head has been turning. It got to a point where I got a sore neck. I had to go to a massage parlor. I got a lot more than a massage. Good lord! It is amazing what you get for a sore neck in the city of angels. It starts off as a sensual massage and before you know it you are shouting. What's my name?. Whose your daddy?

When I come to the city of angels I had high expectations. I expected to live the high flying lifestyle with booty shaking women. The reality is that you end up sleeping on a bunk bed. If you are lucky with a foreign chick who cannot speak English. I expected to be with the ladies of the red carpet but the realty is that you end up getting laid by hookers on Santa Monica Boulevard. Yes I said it. If you want to come to Hollywood just aim for a regular fat chick to avoid major disappointment. Fat girls maybe hard to find. I like a woman with some meat on her. The skinny women once you get your hands on the boob job that is it. It is all bone from there. I like it when my hands have something to do. Something to hold on to you know what I mean. You do not want to end up inspecting the chest job. That is right. That is what I am calling it now. You start to see the scars on both sides. The idea is you must have a lot to do so you miss all that.

I have always wanted to write a book. The one that keeps coming to my head is one called ducking lessons for rapper fifty cent. The brother was hit by nine bullets. Surely after three bullets hit you must duck. President Bush ducked those shoes like a professional. He kind of impressed me. You do not want a President that gets bit up by some punk throwing shoes. Fifty cent must have been high on something. When you are high the reaction time is slow. When you see people that do not like you coming with guns run for your life. If they start shooting duck brother duck. I think he was so high this is how he was thinking. I see people that I have beef with coming towards me. They do not look happy at all. They might be mad at me well maybe. Bang! Bang! Bang!. Oh man three bullets have just struck me. Why do people shoot at others. Don't they know it is painful. Bang! Bang! Bang!. Bullet number six just hit me. There might be something serious these guys are upset about. What could that be really?. I remember I might have said something mean to that guy. Bang! Bang! Bang!. Bullet number nine just hit me. I think it is time to duck. Wait a minute they are close. I think it is time to run.

The following is just a public service announcement. It is not meant to be funny. When a girl has small breasts you must have a big ass. It balances out so you can maintain your value. If you have small tits and have no ass girls that is pretty bad. You must be prepared to take any guy or girl that can have you. This is usually caused by refusal to eat or as they call it in America dieting. We do not have that problem in Africa. Our problem is finding food.

My name is Charles Chiyangwa and one of my fantasies is sleeping with famous women. I would like to take off their clothes. Slide down their Prada underwear and sleep with them. Yes that is what I would like to do. That is some good stuff. I apologize if there are any famous women hearing me say this. If you are horny that is not a bad idea.

I don't know about you. I am scared of the future. Technology is moving fast. I have heard people complaining that using the restroom is taking too long. They say it is messing their productivity at work. That is scary to me. What is going to happen is that someone will invent an automatic waste disposal system. That system will require a tube placed up your ass. You plug it in and it sucks everything out in a second. That is so you can go about your business of working yeah right. I think that is a bad invention. It messes up our love lives. Imagine telling your girlfriend your tube is getting in the way.

If you think about it we have sent a man to the moon. We have not been able to invent a solution to the single most important thing that affects us daily. That is preventing cheating in men and in women. Society has not been able to invent a device that would make hundred percent sure that people do not cheat. Maybe the guy who is suppose to invent the technology is busy cheating. The device should be thinner than a strand of hair and placed down there on the sexual organs. Any illegal activity would be recorded and available online to suspicious husbands, wives, boyfriends and girlfriends. That would make divorce court more interesting. People would start showing up with a computer printout of illegal activity as evidence.

I did not understand why everybody is obsessed with skinny women. It is because they are easier to fuck. Everybody big penis small penis can handle skinny women. In case the car breaks down you can carry them on your back. I am not going to mention other things you can do with skinny women. I am not going to go there. I am trying to be family friendly here.

Let me take a minute here to talk about boob terror. Boob terror basically occurs when girls with big boobs terrorize those with small ones. I am here to say girls with small boobs we feel your pain. Although we may wish other things for you. I think you need to be treated with respect. Ohhh!. That is very sensitive of me. Somebody has got to stand up for the little ones.

Fifty percent of marriages are failing. That is a huge problem for me. We have all these new technologies to mess around with. Yet we cannot invent devices to stop the number one cause of marriage failure. Cheating!. Cheating is the number one cause of marriages that fail. It causes families to break up costing the government billions of dollars. Here is a high tech solution to the problem of cheating. When people get married they should submit their D.N.A. The D.N.A. is then embedded to be implanted with hair strand thin devices. These devices are implanted in the married couple's sex organs. For the woman if there is illegal entry by unrecognized D.N.A., the husband would receive a text message alerting him of the violation. He would then use his cell phone and g.p.s. system to track the location of the alleged violation. The husband will have two options. The first is either to go there himself and confront the alleged violator. The other option is to call the penis and virginal violations police to go and take care of the problem. These departments would be formed at all police stations to respond to violations of trust.

The husband and wife should have condoms they use encoded with a number. Something similar to a social security number. If the husband uses these condoms elsewhere wife receives text message alert. If husband uses condoms outside the serial numbers allocated to the marriage, the implanted device on the husband notifies the wife by text message. She can then use g.p.s. and cell phone to track the husband. She will also have an option to go by herself and confront the violator. She can sip a glass of wine while the violations police deal with it. Most women I know will use this option. Women do not want any trouble. Especially if it has to do with another woman suspected of sleeping with their husband. This should end all cheating. Families would be able to stay together. The government saves billions of dollars. Everybody wins. Sounds like a good idea. I know it may not make sense to some people. I know some of you are smart.

This high tech stuff is only for America though. In Africa the scariest thing is nobody knows what happens to you if you cheat. If you sleep with another man's wife get ready for weird stuff to happen to you. One guy started growing a vagina on his forehead courtesy of black magic. A woman I knew grew a penis at the top of her head for sleeping with another woman's husband. A completely normal working guy would start humping a tree so that people would gather. His actions prompted a question. What happened to him? The answer he slept with another man's wife. In one African country the magistrate had to spend a night in prison to hear for himself some alleged night noises. This was after prisoners complained that one of the inmates had a rooster making noise in his stomach. The magistrate confirmed the rooster noises to be genuine. The man then confessed to what he had done. He said he was treated well by a prostitute with a lavish rooster meal and good sex. He then ran away without paying for the service. Buddy if you want to live a good prison life. Learn to pay for services rendered to you. I pay for services especially if they are good. I have had no rooster well in my case lobster scratching my stomach. It goes to show black magic is much more dangerous and lethal than high tech.

On that basis hopefully Africans can use black magic technology to go to the moon. Rumors are that some people have already started going but it has not been made public. One guy claims that he brought back the U.S.A. flag put on the moon by Armstrong. He claims he put an African flag up there. After you read this you might want to keep it hush hush. This information might cause problems. Once again I want to take this opportunity to thank everyone for flying in. Good thing is you did not have to worry about airport security. Get here any way you can. It is all good in my head. What a world?.

I am a Britney Spears fan. I love my Britney. Here is a pop star who decided she is going to live her life despite the paparazzi. She had not cut her hair since she was really young. All kinds of things were growing in there and she cut it. Everybody thought she lost it. If things are growing in your hair and you can feel them move. I think you have the right to cut it. The interesting thing to me is how she rewarded the young men that supported her. The millions of young men that did stuff looking at her pictures. They made Britney millions by buying her albums. The way it was reported in the press is that she forgot her underwear at home. I am sure that is a common problem among women. It has never happened to me. None of the girls I have dated come to me with that situation. Guess what I forgot my underwear at home do you mind?. Besides the concerns about hygiene I do not mind at all.

I was in Amsterdam Holland the land of the truly free. That is what I call the place. They do not just say we are a free country on paper. They let you exercise your freedoms over there. If you want to use drugs thus ok just do so safely. We will provide you with clean niddles at the designated centre. Last time I heard some noble folks over there were trying to form a pedophile association. Imagine having the American Pedophile Association to promote the rights of pedophiles. The right to do what?. I think it also makes sense to form the American pedophile killers association to promote the hunting and killing of pedophiles. This is so extreme it makes me laugh. You just want to say you cannot do that buddy. Apparently yes you can in Holland.

Now you see legal prostitution does not sound bad at all. They view prostitution as a legitimate tax paying profession. I did not understand why that was so until I arrived in Amsterdam. When you drink beer in their restaurant night club slush pot centre you start to get it. For me I think it was the combination of the crossfire because everybody was blazing weed. I think they see similarities in what prostitutes, singers and dancers do. They both use their mouth to make sound while performing their work. They both use leg movement to enhance their performances. You may argue that prostitutes use private parts in performing their work. Well the mouth is not a private part. Although to be fair a private part sometimes enter the mouth. So for the people of this country it does not make sense to discriminate against prostitutes. Singers and dancers use their bodies the same way with minor variations. Truth be told some singers are prostitutes. I mean both men and women. When I heard that I was like these people are smart. Somehow it did not make the same kind of sense once I left the country.

I think God is a complicated guy. He could have made certain things easier. Sex for instance. Why do we have to take our clothes off to have sex? He could have just made sex like a guy puts his finger under her armpits. Yes armpits. It smells the same. Armpits have hair. When a man's finger is in the girl's armpit, an automatic twenty minute orgasm happens. How cool and easy is that?. In the club you could be dancing and have sex right there. That eliminates dating and I don't care. I am not successful at it. The right to bare arms becomes the most discussed topic among women. She showed her arms she is a slut. That is a lot easier. I am pretty sure women are tired of spreading their legs. I can't say that for men and their wieners. I can hear women complaining about something I just said. I know women are saying did you just say use a finger? Are you crazy? They are saying if we make sex easier, why not make it better at the same time. Instead of using a finger on that armpit, why not use the whole hand with a clinched fist. I know how you think.

I have been hearing a lot of black women complaining about white girls taking their few good black men. That is because white girls take care of broke niggers. They fuck their brains out. Now you black women do not want to have anything to do with a broke man. When a broke man makes his money he is back to where he was taken care of. He is not afraid that when the money runs out your ass is gone. It is like you were never there. My suggestion is that black women need to start sleeping with everybody just like white chicks. I mean rich or poor. Otherwise you are going to be stuck at the singles bar with nobody holding your ass. You be waiting for the big money rapper to take you to paradise and live happily ever after. Sisters stop whining and get some strategies going. White men are free. Get you a white man. Broke brothers taken care of by white girls are not coming back to you if they make money. Those brothers make money they are not coming to you. Stop whining about your competition sisters do something. Do what the first black President did. You size up your enemy. You see their weaknesses and you form a strategy. I know you sisters are smart quit whining. The same relationships you despise of gave us the first black President so suck it up. This just crossed my mind.

I brought up the first black President. What does that mean to me?. No jokes here folks. I am getting serious for a moment. I feel I am part of the American story now. The President's father is African. He came here in search of a dream and so did I. For the first time I feel my chances of being invited to the White House Christmas party are better this year. The president is African American. His father is from Kenya Africa. I am from Africa. My chances of eating dinner in the White House are pretty good. My only request is no speeches when I am eating. It is a noble black man request. If he brings a teleprompter to greet me that would freak me out. I kind of want to meet the community organizing guy. Yo wass up type stuff. I have a feeling I am going to meet the American President. I hope I do not have to resort to my old ghetto tactics to meet him. That's getting a bullhorn and shout him out of the white house. I will go there and shout Obama come out!. I want to meet you. That will cause some problems. I hope to get the invitation. I think that will be easy for everyone. There is one thing I hope I will be allowed to do. That is to give the president the first ever presidential swagger award. Boy the guy's got swagger. He has got it. In case you have doubt he is black. He is swagger black. Again the guy is flawed. The kids complained on television that because he was running for president he thought he could leave his bags everywhere. The kids were tripping on his bags. Mr President that is bad. You cannot do that in the white house. I think this is an area I can give the smooth talking black president advice. It doesn't matter who you are, you cannot trip the kids with your bags. This includes anybody running for President in future.

It will be interesting to go back to Washington to meet the American President. The last time I visited Washington the cowboy was in there boy oh boy. There were all kinds of protests in the park overlooking the white house. Remember the cowboy's wanted dead or alive speech for Osama. I will never forget the bring it on chant. I lived in Texas. That is typical cowboy stuff. There is one thing that has always puzzled me though. A couple of years ago the Harporian queen herself declared that this is the one!. My question is how did the harporian queen know that this individual the junior senator from Chicago was going to be President? I do not buy the I felt it stuff. I hope to meet her personally and ask her the dreaded question. How did you know that this junior guy was going to be the President?. She will try to dance around. I will look her in the eyeball. There will be no playing then. When the moment comes I will ask the question. How did you know skinny from Chicago was going to be president? The president elect had to workout after the gavenator of California made fun of his skinny body. That is not cool. Next time we should pass a law under one of our many propositions. That law will prohibit the governor of California from making fun of any presidential candidate. God knows how much we could have got from the president elect. Had he not spent most of his time working out. Dame you gavenator. There was a quick transition from skinny to the rock Obama in a short period of time. Make no mistake about it I support the United States President. Unlike the fat comedian I want him to succeed.

A lot of comedians have complained that the black president is hard to make fun of. It is not easy I admit. We hope he goes to a foreign country and try to open a locked door on camera or something. A good one is if he dances in front of the white house waiting for a guest. The real hip hop dance I mean.

I wanted to write this story as an article for publication in one of the major newspapers. I never got around to it. I thought it would be nice to share it with you tonight. I hear voices in my head. They say all kinds of stuff." "Yes he is African and I am dating him". "Seal is African". "Barack's father is African. I have just said positive things about Africa in succession. That's wishful thinking in today's world.

Africa is Europe's ex girlfriend and that relationship ended badly. Asia has been spreading rumors that Africa has a STD. The reason being that Asia is sleeping with Europe and the last thing Asia wants is to see Europe messing around with Africa again. The thing is Europe is sluttish and has had a relationship with Africa before until Africa cried rape. Those were the good times that Europe has never forgotten. On the other hand Asia is not secure with his manhood. The country has a good supply of Viagra to keep a good showing. Meanwhile America is waiting to fuck whoever is easy. As you can see it is difficult to continue to write my story using this line of thinking without being pornographic. As you can imagine America gets naughty with Europe. Stuff I can not print here. Rumors are also rampant that Africa is messing around with Asian whores. I am now going to tell my story in layman terms. I will try.

Have you ever asked yourself what happened to all the wealth that Africa had when it was colonized those many years ago. The answer is it is still there. The reality is that now Africans are killing each other for it. The coverage of all the wars in Africa has left the impression that nothing good happens in Africa. I don't even think people in America know people get laid in Africa. The average American's instincts kick in when they meet an African. They ask about what they know about Africa. I have been asked about a war in my country even though there is no war. You don't know what to say. If it is a woman you just agree and ask to touch her boob.

I cannot go around giving a history lesson to everybody. That boob will ease my pain. Sometimes I start complaining about spending time without sex because of the problems in my homeland. I think you know what happens next. It is a bad situation. I have to get something out of it. Do not blame me. A brother has to take care of himself in tough times.

Here are the headlines from the newspapers where I come from. They do not help the image. This is real life. It is not a happy ending movie. I am just saying it like it is. These are my peoples so I am not going to comment on these headlines. Here we go.

Inmates use bible as toilet paper.
Man killed for failing to buy beer.
Woman beaten by snake while defecating.
HIV positive beast rapes own mom.
Hitch hikers forced to dig up graves.
Woman carried money spinning lizards.
Man grows female genital organs on face after cheating with a married woman.

Priest won't bless dread locked man's wedding.
Man has pregnant belly after failing to pay prostitute.

White people you can laugh at the headlines it is okay. I am not going to do anything to you. I am just going to remember your face in case we meet outside. I may have questions for you. If I do not like your answer, I may punch you a little in the face. Just a little punch nothing to worry about. Little blood may come out again you can easily wipe that off. Nothing to worry about really.

I have been asked some dumb questions here in America. Somebody comes up to me and asks if I run around with tigers back in Africa?. You don't know were to start. I just play along. Of cause tigers are fun to hang around with especially when they are hungry. You will love them. Then I go I want to take you with me next time I go back to Africa. I am going to take you tiger riding. If I can do it you can do it too. I am going to make you go solo. Only one thing I am going to let you know right now. That is you just make sure the tiger you ride is not hungry. They might have you for lunch.

One girl come up to me and asked me if I got modern clothes upon arrival In America. I had it up to here with that question. I just said to her let me show you what you think. So I took my shirt off, my pants off, my underwear and everything off. At that point I was naked. So this is how we are in Africa. Do you like it? She was like you crazy African. At that point I started jumping up and down to showcase my manhood. The relationship that resulted lasted about two years. It was one of the good ones I have had here.

There are certain stories about the motherland they never show on television. I would like to see a story about an African guy named Gudza Dungwe who drives a Bentley. He made his fortune in the tobacco industry in Africa. He is surrounded by beautiful women. On a Friday night he is on his way to a hip hop club. After the club Mr. Dungwe is going to hit the hotel for an after party. It's all good here in Africa. This is Anderson Cooper reporting for CNN in Africa. I hope to see this one day so I can start having some informed conversations up in here. Gudza Dungwe has a better chance of making the news in America, if he gets drunk and kills two hundred people. Then you have hundreds of press people flying to Africa to cover the Gudza Dungwe massacres two hundred people story. Gudza Dungwe gets laid at the after party will never be covered. If he makes a sex tape then all hell will break loose. Breaking news about the Gudza Dungwe sex tape. Gudza is shown totally naked on the tape and it is amazing footage. The relationship between the motherland and the west has been a complicated one. There has been engagements, marriages, divorces and name calling.

A lot of people especially girls has tried to mimic my African accent. I am just going to let you know something now. Ninety nine point nine percent of girls who have done so have ended up in my bed. Yep next to me in my bed. You can go ahead and make fun of the way I talk. Bring your own blankets because I am kind of short on blankets. Oh I almost forgot an important thing bring regular condoms no female condoms for me .You are coming to a man's house. That means me. Thank you. Thank you for coming. From the team that lives in my head and me thank you. I hope you had a good time tonight. Thank you. God bless you. Good night!!!!!!!.

STAGE LIGHTS FADE AS I WALK AWAY FROM THE STAGE. HOUSE LIGHTS COME UP AMID PEOPLE STARTING TO CHATTER ABOUT THE SHOW.

Encore
I am in my dressing room I think for about five minutes. The crowd has not left. I start to hear people shouting encore! encore! One more! One more!. The stage manager encourages me to go out and just say goodbye for a second time. According to him the crowd just wants to see me for the last time before flying off. I stumbled back on to the stage and immediately started singing.

Verse
I am a Blackman.
I don't do cocaine.
I need some food.
I would rather be fat!

Fat! Fat! Fat!. I would rather be fat.

By the time I repeated the verse the crowd went nuts. Then it just occurred to me that they were laughing. They are laughing!. I could feel tears slowly filling my eyes. I had to say thank you to the audience for their appreciation. Thank you very much. I appreciate the love. You guys are awesome. Guys do not drink too much. You have a job to do. When you get home with the ladies you brought here tonight get busy. I know this is not only about coming here to laugh. If you happen to accidentally drink too much, which I hope you do not do. Please do not puke on the girl. If you do that you will wake up by yourself tomorrow. Wondering what happened?. The comedy was good. I spent some money. Where did she go? Guys because you spent some money tonight, do not walk home with your dick in your hand. I did that one time. I had to beg on my knees. I had to produce a fake tear to get it. Women do not act surprised when we come for it. Like you thought there was an alternative ending to the story. As I lay naked on the bed waiting for my man, he suddenly flew out the window never to return. Oh! what a wasted chance. Yeah right.

I hope you do not make the decision to marry your lady tonight. It is not a good day. You have been laughing all night and you are drunk. She will think it was a joke. Especially if you cannot remember some things that happened tonight. Then what happened next? Well then you asked me to marry you.

As you have noticed I do not have a tattoo. I am scared of tattoo remorse. What do you do if you discover after a few days you no longer want it. You cannot rub it off. The only useful tattoo really is the lower back tattoo women have. It has got residual value. It is viewable during pleasure. Every night the woman knows it is serving a purpose. For your eyes only.

It is difficult to get people's attention at a party. I devised a good way to get people's attention. You walk up to them and say your car is on fire. When they give you the look you tell them just kidding!. The one I like is when I tell someone you have broken your legs. They look at me almost crying asking how?. Then I go just kidding you are standing on them. This one almost got me in trouble. I told this one dude your wife cheated on you today. When I said my joke the wife was across the room. By the time I finished she was walking towards her husband. Upon seeing her he immediately started choking her. By the time I said I was kidding I had a scene on my hands. In the scene a woman struggling to breathe.

I did not realize how professionals can sometimes be very competitive. I walked up to a professional doctor having a conversation with his friends. I told him he had a fake degree. Before I said I was kidding all the others started leaving. I could hear them saying they knew it. The other doctor said we should have checked him out before allowing him into our group. Well there I was standing with a furious doctor telling him I was just kidding. This one I just thought about but I do not think I will ever do. Walking up to a group of women at a party and tell one of them she got fake boobs. I am kind of scared of what will be thrown at me before saying I am just kidding. I can imagine drinks being thrown at me. I think anything they can get their hands on. It is also a good way to be thrown out of a party.

I have a feeling something good is going to happen to me. I feel it. I am scared that I am just going to fart. That is a great feeling because you can feel it too. What I am talking about is different. It feels different. I just hope it is not some booty shaking chick coming in front of me crying for free sex. That is great for a moment but my feeling is more like for eternity. I certainly hope it is not my death. That feeling maybe great for some but I love life. It has been a privilege to live this life even though I am poor. Anything sexual is exciting but it is not forever. What is going to happen to me?.

Women wonder why men like porn so much. Let me tell you the reason is that porn looks clean all the time. In real life sex is not always that clean. I always get the question what do you like in a woman?. What I like is a very simple request. Your bra and panties have to match. I cannot handle greens and yellows black and whites. That is a deal breaker for me. I remember after the club one night going to a twenty four hour store to buy this girl matching underwear. To make matters worse I could not find a match for the purple pink bra she had on. They had the material that matched for sale. I bought the material and found myself sewing underwear in the middle of the night. This was so I could sleep with this playboy model looking chick.

Good news for all you women out there. I was watching television the other day and a Japanese guy has the fastest world record for taking his clothes off. He does it in about seven point three seconds. I guess you can call him the fastest pant dropper. He is got the record but I have met women that are faster. You look away for one second and when you look back at her it is hey!. It does not happen to everybody. You have to be lucky or have lots of money. I mean lots of it. For most of us you have to allocate ten minutes to pull your girl out of the skinny jeans. Women must be enjoying this story. The fastest pant dropper is a Japanese man. I can see a lot of women breathing a sigh of relief. I am not quite sure if his skills are of any use though. Certainly not with women. Do not take my word for it. I may be wrong. Maybe you women want a ready man. Well if that is the case you might want to catch a plane to Japan. Thank you very much good night. I am out of here.

As I am walking off the stage I look back. I see a beautiful scene unfolding. People start to fly out of the arena. They are using their hands as wings to fly home. I see them leave in pairs or in groups. What is amazing is that everybody is smiling and happy. People of all walks of life. I begin to wonder whether this is real or just my imagination!.

Back on Hollywood boulevard I am looking at the scene of the crime. I walk by here everyday. I have done all kinds of activities trying to remember. I hope one day I will completely remember what happened here. Hollywood boulevard 2.00pm. I am out. God bless the world!.

www.ingramcontent.com/pod-product-compliance
Lightning Source LLC
Chambersburg PA
CBHW020512030426
42337CB00011B/343